ENVIRONMENTAL DISASTERS

Los Alamos

Wildfires

by Nichol Bryan

WORLD ALMANAC® LIBRARY

Please visit our web site at: www.worldalmanaclibrary.com
For a free color catalog describing World Almanac® Library's list of high-quality books and multimedia programs, call 1-800-848-2928 (USA) or 1-800-387-3178 (Canada). World Almanac® Library's fax: (414) 332-3567.

Library of Congress Cataloging-in-Publication Data

Bryan, Nichol, 1958-
   Los Alamos: wildfires / by Nichol Bryan.
     p. cm. — (Environmental disasters)
   Summary: Describes the events surrounding the wildfire that raged in New Mexico in 2000 and the resulting debate over the policy of prescribed burning, or purposely setting fires as a means of forest management.
   Includes bibliographical references and index.
   ISBN 0-8368-5507-8 (lib. bdg.)
   ISBN 0-8368-5514-0 (softcover)
   1. Wildfires—New Mexico—Los Alamos Region—Juvenile literature. 2. Prescribed burning—New Mexico—Los Alamos Region—Juvenile literature. [1. Wildfires—New Mexico. 2. Prescribed burning.] I. Title.
II. Series.
SD421.23.B78   2003
363.37'9—dc21   2003053536

First published in 2004 by
World Almanac® Library
330 West Olive Street, Suite 100
Milwaukee, WI 53212 USA

Copyright © 2004 by World Almanac® Library.

Produced by Lownik Communication Services
Cover design and page production: Heidi Bittner-Zastrow
Picture researcher: Jean Lownik
World Almanac® Library art direction: Tammy Gruenewald
World Almanac® Library series editor: Carol Ryback

Photo Credits: Cover, 18, 20, 22 (t), 23, 25, 30, 40, 43 © Rick Wilking REUTERS; 4, Heidi Bittner-Zastrow; 5, 31(t), © Steven G. Smith, Albuquerque Tribune; 6(b), Michael Caulfield © REUTERS; 6(t), AFP PHOTO/NOAA © CORBIS; 7, © Lynda Richardson/CORBIS; 8, Photo courtesy of Los Alamos National Laboratory; 9, © SACHS RON/CORBIS SYGMA; 10, 16, 22(b), 26, © Raymond Gehman/CORBIS; 11, © Royalty-Free/CORBIS; 12, © George H. H. Huey/CORBIS; 13, © Premium Stock/CORBIS; 14(b), © Douglas Faulkner/CORBIS; 14(t), © CORBIS; 15, © KJ Historical/CORBIS; 19, © Gary Braasch/CORBIS; 21, © Joseph Sohm; ChromoSohm Inc./CORBIS; 24, © Randy Faris/CORBIS; 27, 29, © Toby Jorrin, Albuquerque Tribune; 28, 33, 34, © REUTERS; 31(b), 32, 37, 41, Photo by Andrea Booher/FEMA News Photo; 36, © AP Photo/Albuquerque Journal, Kitty Clark; 38, © Michael J. Gallegos/Albuquerque Tribune; 42, Martone Sara/CORBIS SYGMA

Printed in the United States of America

1 2 3 4 5 6 7 8 9 07 06 05 04 03

Cover: On May 11, 2000, the Cerro Grande Fire threatened the Los Alamos National Laboratory, one of the United States's largest nuclear facilities. The Cerro Grande Fire is the official name of the fire that consumed part of the city of Los Alamos, New Mexico.

Contents

Los Alamos

NEW MEXICO

Introduction

The Fire**Storm**

It was a perfect storm of fire. Driven by 50-mile-per-hour (80-kilometer-per-hour) winds, fed by thirty years of dead, bone-dry logs and brush, it consumed everything in its path. It was racing down on a community of eighteen thousand people, and there was little firefighters could do but get out of the way. Worse, it was heading straight for one of the nation's biggest nuclear research facilities, raising the fear of radioactive smoke that might spread out over three states.

The fire burned 45,000 acres (18,000 hectares) of wilderness and destroyed more than two hundred

A plume of fire engulfs a tree and a home near Arkansas Avenue in Los Alamos, New Mexico.

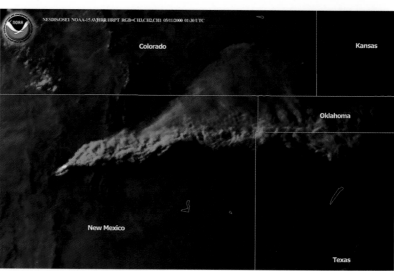

A National Oceanic and Atmospheric Administration (NOAA) satellite image released May 11, 2000 shows the Cerro Grande Fire burning out of control. Smoke streams across northeastern New Mexico and into neighboring states.

homes and businesses. Fifteen hundred firefighters fought the blaze, which did more than $1 billion in damage. The fire was so huge, it was seen from space.

The wildfire that swept through Los Alamos, New Mexico, in May 2000 wasn't the biggest the American West has seen in many years of fire seasons. Nor was it the deadliest. But it did rivet the nation's attention. That's because unlike most fires in America's forests, this one was no accident. It was set on purpose by the National Park Service.

The fiery blaze brought America's attention to a controversy that had been smoldering behind the scenes of U.S. forest management for years. The idea that the federal government would deliberately set fires in a national park came as a shock to many, even though the policy of "controlled burns" had been in place for decades. A generation of Americans raised with images of Smokey Bear and *Bambi* cartoons regarded fire as the worst possible thing that could happen in a forest.

Now they viewed television images of people fleeing before the fire and homeowners tearfully watching their

Los Alamos victims of the Cerro Grande Fire visit their devastated home on May 14, 2000. It was their first chance after the fire to see what — if anything — was left standing.

homes go up in smoke. If the fire reached the nearby nuclear research laboratory, it posed the threat of nuclear contamination and a risk that our atomic secrets would not be safe. The idea that a government program caused this scenario angered many people and lawmakers.

The fire — called a prescribed burn — was purposely set as part of the forestry management plan for Cerro Grande Peak to help *prevent* severe, uncontrollable blazes. In fact, environmentalists and forestry experts had recommended more prescribed burns for the area, maintaining that such fires were important to preserve the natural ecosystem of wild lands.

A worker leaves the Blackwater National Wildlife Refuge in Cambridge, Maryland, after starting a prescribed burn. Refuge managers routinely set certain areas ablaze to help preserve natural ecosystems and to prevent severe, uncontrollable fires.

Los Alamos: The Secret City

Los Alamos was founded as the home of the Manhattan Project — a top-secret World War II program that built the first atomic bomb. In 1943, the U.S. War Department housed scores of the world's top physicists in this secluded, top-secret city. Thousands of trained workers were also on hand to help fabricate the bombs and run the reactors that produced nuclear materials. All were forbidden to tell anyone where they were living and working, or what they were doing. It was only after the first atomic bombs fell on Japan at the end of WWII in August 1945 that outsiders were even aware of the existence of Los Alamos.

Although Los Alamos became a civilian town after the war, the weapons research facility, Los Alamos National Laboratory, continued to operate. The nuclear laboratory stored large amounts of radioactive materials and had several on-site pits where nuclear waste had been dumped. In the 1940s and 1950s, before scientists fully understood the dangers of radioactivity, liquid radioactive waste was simply poured onto the ground near the lab to drain away. This practice contaminated tons of soil with radioactivity. It is still radioactive fifty years later.

An aerial view shows the campus of the Los Alamos National Laboratory.

"Priority One"

"Saving lives and property is, and will remain, priority one . . . We're reducing the risk of fire on more than 2.4 million acres (970,000 ha) a year — a fivefold increase since 1994.

We want to work with communities to expand these efforts, in an environmentally sensitive way, particularly in those areas at greatest risk of wildfire."

— President Bill Clinton, September 2000

Since the beginning of the twentieth century, people of the United States have undergone an enormous change in their attitudes toward fire. The American West, once a wild land to be conquered, was settled. Americans now had property to protect and resources to develop. People building homes on the edge of the wilderness expected to be kept safe from fire. The timber industry wanted the millions of acres of national forests protected for future harvests. Americans went from regarding wildfire as a natural, unavoidable force to viewing it as an enemy.

In the last fifty years or so, scientists began to question the wisdom behind the policy on fire prevention in undeveloped areas. They discovered that many habitats *needed* regular fires to stay healthy. Forestry experts realized that years of preventing smaller fires caused even bigger and harder-to-fight fires.

That evidence led the same federal agency that invented Smokey Bear to do the unthinkable — that is, purposely set fires on public lands. People who lived near the land where fires were set questioned the practice from its onset. And television images of Los Alamos in flames created a national debate on prescribed burns. The Department of the Interior banned the practice for months, while federal officials weathered blistering attacks at Congressional hearings.

Since the fire — officially known as the Cerro Grande Fire — U.S. public opinion has straddled both sides of the wildfire debate. After the destruction

Sonny Stoddard, Jr., of Thomasville, Georgia, has practiced setting prescribed burns on his 1,000-acre (405 ha) plantation for more than fifty years. Some call him the "Dean of Prescribed Fire."

at Los Alamos, many called for sharp limits on the government's ability to manage controlled burns. But after another devastating fire season in 2002, people began to see the dangers of letting dead, dry wood and brush build up in the forest. Some called for a more aggressive program of prescribed burns. Others pushed for increased logging of dead and dying trees.

In the end, the problem of what to do about wildfires is more than just a question of forestry and firefighting techniques. It is a question of politics.

In order to reach a national agreement on how to prevent fires and preserve forests, people in the United States need to change the way they think about fire itself.

Chapter 1

Fighting Fire
with Fire

It is an area of wild, natural beauty. No wonder humans have wanted to live there for thousands of years.

The 33,000 acres (13,000 ha) now known as Bandelier National Monument sprawl across north central New Mexico, surrounded by the Santa Fe National Forest. This wilderness includes nearly everything nature has to offer, from arid canyons and rocky cliffs to vast mountains covered with pine forest. Rising over everything, Cerro Grande Peak reaches 10,000 feet (3,000 meters) into the sky

Five hundred years before Christopher Columbus arrived in the Western Hemisphere, this rich, wild land and volcanic soil attracted the ancient Pueblo (PWAY bvloh) people. They farmed and hunted in the Bandelier region until disappearing in the 1500s. The Pueblo left behind cave dwellings and hundreds of adobe structures, including a three-story "apartment" building in Frijoles Canyon.

A full moon shines over the rugged, wild beauty of the Sangre de Cristo mountains near Taos, New Mexico.

Bandelier National Monument in north central New Mexico features sheer-walled canyons, mesas, and ancestral Pueblo dwellings. A popular trail leads hikers through Frijoles Canyon. Bandelier includes more than 23,000 acres (9,300 ha) of designated wilderness.

Archeologists have found traces of the cotton cloth the Pueblo wove and the beautiful pottery they made from the local clay.

Fire was a natural part of the Pueblo's world, as it had always been for Native Americans. Wildfires caused by lightning would sweep through the surrounding forests. These ancient people knew that fire wasn't always a bad thing. It not only heated their homes, cooked their food, and hardened their clay pots, but also was good for the land. Fire cleared out dead and sickly plants and trees, clearing the way for new growth. Wild plants used as food grew better after a fire. Hunting was better after a fire, too, because the fresh fodder helped the deer population increase. In fact, evidence indicates that Native Americans set their own fires for thousands of years.

The Pueblo had been gone for centuries by the time the first white people stumbled on the settlement at Frijoles Canyon in 1880. Much else had also changed in the American West. European settlers had spread out across

Harvested logs dwarf a worker inspecting lumber. The U.S. timber industry supplies the world with everything from paper products, to posts and poles, to building supplies, to surfboards and hockey sticks.

the continent. They farmed the grasslands and trapped and logged in the forests. Most of these new Americans cared little for the ancient knowledge of the Native peoples they drove out. To the white settlers, wildfire was a danger to life and property — a hazard to be prevented. They saw the fires set by Native Americans as one more reason to distrust and fear them.

As the twentieth century drew near, America's view of its western wilderness began to change. People no longer regarded the West as a limitless territory to be conquered. Instead, they became concerned with preserving not only the wild beauty of the West, but also its vast timber resources, on which the growing nation was coming

to depend. Congress set aside huge tracts of land as national parks and forest preserves. The conservation movement had begun.

Congress formed the U.S. Forest Service (USFS) in 1905 to develop and protect the country's forest preserves. From the very beginning, the USFS dedicated itself to preventing fire on the country's wild lands. Forest Service officials felt that fires destroyed standing trees and burned fragile new trees, preventing the next generation of forest from developing.

In 1910, something happened that changed this goal into an obsession — one that would become a national obsession.

It was called the Big Blowup.

In August of 1910, strong winds blowing over the Rocky Mountains fanned wildfires into firestorms. The result was an arc of fire stretching from California all the way to Minnesota. The massive fire destroyed more than 3 million acres (1.2 million ha) of forest and grassland. As the fire roared across the continent, some Americans thought the world was coming to an end.

About nine thousand men (a gigantic number of firefighters for the early twentieth century) struggled against the blaze. Seventy-eight of them were killed, often when they were suddenly surrounded by flames that spread instantly and unexpectedly because of the strong winds. Army troops were called in to help control the flames. In the end, the Big Blowup cost $1 million to fight — roughly $23 million dollars today.

The fire that burned this acreage in New Mexico's Lincoln National Forest is the same one that swept much of the western United States in 1910. Firefighters found a bear cub clinging to a tree. They named him Smokey.

While fighting the fire, Army firefighters found a bear cub clinging to a tree, his fur singed by the flames. They hauled the cub from the woods and nursed him back to health. The

A Controversial Practice
"Resistance to change remains. Even today, when most ecologists acknowledge the need to use Indian-type fires to restore a wildland mosaic of forest and grassland at various successional stages, the practice remains controversial, especially among fire control professionals."

— Gerald W. Williams,
USDA Forest Service historian

little bear recovered and became a mascot for western firefighters.

They named him Smokey.

The story of the Big Blowup, and of Smokey Bear, riveted the nation's attention. Voters demanded better protection for wildlands, and for their own property. The Forest Service vowed never to let a fire get so out of hand again. The formed a new rule, called the "ten o'clock rule." They vowed to extinguish any fire in the nation's forests by 10 A.M. the following morning. This policy guided firefighting for the rest of the century.

In World War II, Americans became even more fixated on the idea of preventing fires. The government launched a campaign to convince people that forests were strategic resources the country needed to win the war. Propaganda posters compared being careless with fire to helping the Germans and Japanese. In 1944, Smokey Bear became the focus of a government fire-prevention campaign that became the longest running public service ad series in history.

Two years before the launch of the Smokey Bear campaign, Walt Disney produced a popular feature cartoon *Bambi* had shown the horrifying impact of forest fires on woodland creatures. An entire generation of children learned to view fire as inherently dangerous — even evil.

As the public campaign for fire prevention caught on, USFS scientists

began to have a new appreciation of fire. They were learning that moderate fires did not really hurt some types of forests. In fact, scientists were starting to realize that some forest habitats needed regular burns to stay healthy.

Ponderosa pines, for instance, have thick bark and deep roots to help them survive fires. As the tree gets taller, the lower branches fall off, so that fires can't climb to the tops of the trees. Ponderosa forests often have a layer of grass that catches fire easily. Grass fires don't hurt the trees. Instead, they clear the ground

---

The public awareness campaign featuring Smokey Bear began in 1944. It is the longest-running public service ad series in U.S. history.

PLEASE!

Only you can prevent forest fires

GRANT VILLAGE   2
GRAND TETON N.P.   29
JACKSON WYO.   79

OLD FAITHFUL   17
WEST YELLOWSTONE 47

A firefighter in Yellowstone National Park, Wyoming, walks past a directional sign in a burned-out forest after the 1988 Shoshone fire.

Restoring the Natural Role of Fire

"Wildland fire will be used to protect, maintain and enhance resources and, as nearly as possible, be allowed to function in its natural ecological role."

— Federal Wildland Policy, 1995

for new Ponderosa seedlings.

Lodgepole pines produce cones that won't release seeds until they are opened by fire. Once a blaze moves through, the cones blanket the surrounding soil with up to ten years' worth of seeds. Lodgepoles also need regular fires to thin out the seedlings so that the surviving trees grow better.

In the 1960s and 1970s, scientists began to increase their understanding of the concept of ecology — the idea that any natural region is a delicate balance of many different factors, and that changing even one factor can cause a big impact on the entire system. With this new view of nature, scientists with the USFS and other agencies that controlled wild lands reached a new conclusion about fire: that sometimes it was necessary to allow fires to burn — controlled, contained, but not immediately put out — to best protect and promote the nation's forests. And, sometimes USFS workers needed to set those fires.

By the end of the twentieth century, the change in thinking about fire was complete. The Federal Wildland Fire Management Policy adopted by the U.S. government in 1995 said that agencies should use controlled fires to restore forests to health. In fact, a 1999 government report blamed the former policy of putting out all fires immediately for causing "an increasing number of large, intense, uncontrollable and catastrophically destructive wildfires." The report said that Western forests would run the risk of huge fires until the year 2015.

But after almost one hundred years of campaigning against forest fires, the public was not so easily convinced. For instance, in 1988, the National Park Service allowed some natural fires in Yellowstone National Park to burn

"The Fundamental Obligation"
"The necessity of preventing losses from forest fires requires no discussion. It is the fundamental obligation of the Forest Service and takes precedence over all other duties and activities."
— Henry Graves, Chief of the U.S. Forest Service, writing in 1913

themselves out. Fires swept through half of the popular park while rangers looked on. It was an early experiment in using fire to improve the health of a forest and reduce the risk of bigger fires later on. But the lack of action angered many people, who claimed it was just one more sign that then-President Ronald Reagan cared nothing about the environment.

Despite the uproar, the USFS, the National Park Service (NPS), and other federal and state agencies continued to expand the use of controlled burning. In 1994, the agency used controlled or prescribed burns on 385,000 acres (156,000 ha) of public land. By 1999, the year before the Cerro Grande Fire, that number increased to 2 million acres (800,000 ha).

One reason people objected to the idea of controlled burns was that more and more of them were living at the edge of the forest. In the West, wooded land on scenic mountains had become hot properties for home builders. In trying

Firefighters hose down a house to prevent sparks from the still-smoldering Cerro Grande Fire from igniting it.

controlled burns sometimes got out of hand. In July 1999, gusty winds caused a fire set by the federal Bureau of Land Management (BLM) in northern California to burn out of control in a populated area. The fire burned twenty-three homes and caused $1.7 million in damage. Investigators claimed the BLM failed to properly warn or protect the local homeowners.

to keep as much of the natural setting as possible, home builders left many trees close to houses. The perimeters of the forests that were becoming the most populated were the ones where fire prevention was a high priority. Many older communities built up decades of dead trees and brush, all waiting for a spark. As a result, those forests that were long overdue for a burn were the same ones where the most lives and developed property were at risk.

As careful as foresters tried to be,

The next year, government agencies again prepared to use fire to fight fire. Conditions were critical. The U.S. Department of the Interior, which controlled the Forest Service, estimated that about 24 million acres (9.7 million ha) of forest in the West were at risk for catastrophic fire. As the fire season rolled around, Western foresters never dreamed that the most destructive fire would be one they set themselves.

Chapter 2

Begging
To Burn

The forest around Cerro Grande Peak was just begging to burn.

Thanks to the policy of fire prevention and control that the nation had followed, by May 2000 the forests in Bandelier National Monument around the city of Los Alamos, New Mexico, had not seen a fire in thirty years. Woodlands were filled with dead trees and dry undergrowth. Many of the dead trees were still standing or leaning against other trees. In case of a fire, the standing trees could carry the flames up to the forest canopy, where it could spread even more quickly.

A severe drought in the region had made this fuel bone dry. The Los Alamos area had gotten less than

Old-growth forests are beautiful, but dead trees and dry undergrowth provide fuel for fire.

one-fifth of its normal moisture the winter before. Now the dead logs were drier than oven-dried lumber sold at local hardware stores.

The NPS felt it was time to act before things got any worse. With several communities — including the Los Alamos National Laboratory — in the area at risk, an uncontrolled fire could be a disaster. Foresters decided that a controlled burn would head off a catastrophe.

A prescribed burn always calls for careful planning. Mike Powell, who had just started his job as Assistant Fire Management Officer at Bandelier, began to produce a Wildland Fire Situation Analysis in February. The USFS must complete a Wildland Fire Situation Analysis whenever it plans a prescribed burn. The analysis included a discussion of the reasons for the burn, as well as the best, safest way to carry it out. Communities and agencies that could be affected by the burn had to be notified of the analysis before the burn could proceed.

In the case of this particular burn, many people were consulted. The list included managers of the Bandelier National Monument and the Santa Fe National Forest that surrounded it. State and county officials were notified, as were managers at the Los Alamos National Laboratory and the U.S. Department of Energy, which runs the nuclear facility. Two Native American communities, the San Ildefonso and Santa Clara Pueblos, were also on the list. So was Baca Land and Cattle Company, a huge ranch that bordered the prescribed burn zone.

A tree explodes in flames as the Cerro Grande Fire rages through the Santa Fe National Forest on May 15, 2000.

Not everybody was enthusiastic about Powell's plan. Several officials wondered why Powell was proposing a controlled fire at a time when camp fires were restricted at the national parks because of the dry conditions. The Forest Service offered to include the Baca Ranch in the burn zone, but the owners there said no. However, USFS policy simply requires that people be informed of the burn plan — they do not have to approve of it. So the burn went on, although with the Baca Ranch was left out.

The plan called for the fire to be started near the top of Cerro Grande. The location was important, because fire burns downhill slower than it burns uphill. The burn would be conducted at night, to make it easier for crews to see the progress of the fire. The plan called for fire teams to do a small test burn, to make sure the fire would behave the way it was expected to with the wind and weather conditions. The teams would then burn parallel "blacklines" on either side of the burn zone, which ran down the south side of the mountain. These wide areas of burned material were supposed to keep the fire from spreading outside the prescribed burn zone.

At about 7:20 P.M. on Thursday, May 4, 2000, Powell met with a team of twenty fire personnel atop Cerro Grande Peak. They started the test fire, and let it burn for forty minutes. Everything went as planned; the fire burned at the rate and in the direction the crew had predicted. Powell gave the go-ahead to start the blacklining.

Using torch guns, crews moved down to create the first blackline, on the northeast side of the burn area.

"The Wind Killed Us on This One"

"This fire has experienced some severe wind events that were not totally forecasted. That was the variable that killed us on this one."

— Tom Zimmerman,
NPS fire scientist

Loree Lynch (l) weeps while holding her daughter Michelle at a Mother's Day service for victims of the Cerro Grande Fire. Lynch's home was not damaged in the fire, but she was not allowed to return to her home for five days.

"Awful"
"It was a wonderful place to live. It's terrible to think about what's happening there. Awful."

— Los Alamos resident, Loretta Baldridge, whose home was destroyed in the Cerro Grande Fire

Normally, blacklines are made by allowing the fire to burn a path, and then putting it out on both sides of the path. This provides a safe boundary before the main fire begins. But the fire crews faced slow going that night. After a while, Powell decided to put out only the outside of the blackline, and let the other side continue to spread into the burn zone.

By 10:00 P.M., Powell and his crew were finished with the blackline on the northeast side of the burn zone. Powell began to walk back to the top of the peak. When he got there, trouble was waiting. The fire had burned through the blackline and was moving into the burn zone faster than expected. When the rest of the blackline crew got to the area, they were able to put out the blaze that had escaped the blackline.

The crews then went to work creating the blackline on the other side of the burn zone. Again, going was slow. It was 2:30 A.M. on May 5 by the time the second blackline was finished. Fire crews were exhausted after six hours of hot work in the rugged terrain. Mike Powell sent most of the crew to their housing trailers to get some sleep. A small group, headed by Paul Gleason, a wildland fire management specialist for the NPS, stayed behind to keep an eye on the fire overnight.

A firefighter uses a drip torch fueled with jellied gasoline (napalm) to ignite roadside grasses in Boise National Forest, Idaho, in 1995.

On May 12, 2000, the famous Zuni Indian firefighters arrived at the Pajarito Mountain Ski Area west of Los Alamos to protect the ski lodge from burning. This group is only one of many "hotshot" firefighting teams sent to help with the Los Alamos wildfires.

Worn out, Powell went to his office. He was worried that keeping this burn controlled was going to take more people than he had on hand. He called a dispatcher to order twenty more firefighters and a helicopter as backup for the next morning. The dispatcher told him to call back in the morning. Then Powell tried to get some sleep himself.

Mike Powell didn't get much rest that night. Less than three hours after he turned in, Paul Gleason was there, waking him up. The fire was burning faster than anybody had expected. It had already burned below the blacklines on the burn zone's south end. Gleason told Powell that the backup crew had better be there fast. Powell got back on the phone to the dispatcher.

What happened next seemed minor at the time, but it would turn out to be one of the big mysteries of the Cerro Grande Fire. Powell later said that he got no answer when he called the dispatcher. The dispatcher said that people were on duty at the time, but they never got a call from Powell.

One way or the other, the message that the burn crew needed help didn't get through until a half hour later, when a supervisor called Powell to find out what was going on. In any case, the backup fire crew did not arrive until late that morning.

The dispatch supervisor let officials at the Santa Fe National Forest know that the blaze at Cerro Grande was starting to get out of hand. He asked whether they wanted to declare that the controlled burn had become a wildland fire. Once the fire was officially declared a wildland fire, park officials could request more crews and equipment to fight it. The declaration would put the communities in the area on notice that the fire had gotten out of control. The NPS decided to hold off declaring a wildland fire.

At 10:30 A.M., a helicopter arrived at the fire scene. It dropped off two more firefighters and then flew off to get a bucket, so it could begin dropping water directly on the fire. By 11:00 A.M., the twenty-person firefighting team known as the "Santa Fe Hotshots," showed up at the fire. The reinforcements arrived in the nick of time. The fire was starting to burn its way over the northeast blackline again, and crews were having a hard time getting it back under control.

Paul Gleason, who had taken over as fire boss from Mike Powell, called for another twenty-person crew. He also

Firestorms occur when a fire becomes so large and intense that it creates its own weather patterns. Strong winds rushing inward at the base feed columns of rising hot air and sustain the firestorm.

"A Real Catastrophe"
"Everything is being done that can be done. And yet, we may just be seeing the beginning of what is a real catastrophe."

— New Mexico Governor Gary Johnson

Utah firefighter Tyler Monroe pauses in the bottom of Santa Clara Canyon. Firefighters hoped that the blackline would prevent the Cerro Grande Fire from crossing the creek in the canyon's bottom.

called for an air tanker — a plane with enormous tanks that hold special fire-suppressant chemicals that are dropped on a fire.

All afternoon, the fire picked up speed. It was burning so rapidly that fire crews on the site couldn't keep it under control. Even though the air tanker dropped its first load by about 4:00 P.M. that afternoon, Gleason knew he needed more fire-fighting muscle, and there was only one way to get it. He officially declared the prescribed burn a wildland fire.

The Physics of Fire

To understand how firefighters tackle a forest fire, you need to know the basics of fire itself. Three things — fuel, oxygen, and heat — are necessary to start a blaze and keep it going. The

Cerro Grande Fire had plenty of all three. The fuel came from decades of dead, dry trees and brush that choked the forests in the area. Oxygen came in the form of wind — winds that were starting to gust higher than NPS officials had predicted. And heat was provided by the NPS crews themselves when they started the controlled burn. As the fire grew larger, it grew hotter, and spread more rapidly.

When fires reach a certain size, they can create their own weather patterns. Heated air at the center of the fire rises quickly, creating a suction at the base of the fire. This suction draws in cooler air from around the base of the fire. The winds that rush in bring more oxygen to the fire, so it burns even hotter and faster. The cycle is called a firestorm, and when it happens, the fire

Firefighter Kimberly Enjady walks with a drip torch at a controlled burn on the Mescalero Apache Indian Reservation in New Mexico. Reservation forests are filled with grasslands that would present a hazard to local housing if the grass is not periodically burned. For centuries, many Native Americans have believed that fire is good for the land.

starts to take on a life of its own.

To fight the fire, crews attempt to remove one or more of the three elements that keep it going. They can rob the fire of fuel by burning areas in its path, so the blaze doesn't cross the blackline. They can lower the temperature of the fire by dropping water on it. Water also removes the third element — oxygen. Firefighters use other techniques to choke off the fire's air supply. On the ground, they beat down smaller blazes with shovels, or spray it with fire retardants. Air tankers can drop retardant chemicals from above. The chemicals work by depriving the fire of oxygen.

As more and more crews and equipment arrived at the fire, firefighters struggled to get the blaze under control. But winds were carrying the fire fast.

Huge clouds of smoke billowed up from the hundreds of acres that were ablaze. By Sunday, May 7, 2000, the surrounding communities became aware that the fire was out of control. Worse, it was heading straight for Los Alamos — and the Los Alamos National Lab.

Nervous homeowners followed news reports. Would fire crews be able to stop the blaze that was approaching their backyards? Or would they be forced to flee — and abandon everything they owned to the blaze?

Chapter 3

"It Should Never **Have Happened**"

Perched on a 7,600-foot (2,300-m) mesa (MAY sah) the town of Los Alamos had an excellent view of the disaster racing toward it.

The population of top-secret Los Alamos — founded in the early 1940s to house the scientists and workers who built the atomic bomb — grew from one thousand five hundred in January 1943 to five thousand seven hundred in January 1945. After World War II, the secret was out and the town continued

A view from the roof of the Los Alamos Library shows flames dancing across the tops of trees.

to grow. By 2000, the Los Alamos National Laboratory nuclear weapons lab employed about seven thousand of the town's eighteen thousand inhabitants. Schools, parks and homes had sprung up on the mesa, surrounded by the forests of Bandelier National Monument and Santa Fe National Forest.

All of that was at risk from the fire that in three days had burned 1,500 acres (607 ha) of woodland. Only Los Alamos Canyon, a steep, heavily wooded ravine that ran west of Los Alamos blocked the fire's progress. National Park Service officials agreed that if the fire made it into that canyon,

"It Should Never Have Happened"
"It should never have happened. That's the only thing I can say unless you want me to curse."

— Gail Bolger, who was forced out of her Los Alamos home

they would have no choice but to evacuate Los Alamos. On Monday, May 8, 2000, the NPS recommended that people on the west side of town seek safety. About three thousand residents left their homes. Los Alamos National Lab told employees to stay away, and many businesses and schools in the area closed.

People in Los Alamos nervously watched the fire and started packing their things. At the same time, they began to ask some angry questions. How was it that

Homeowner Mary Sandoval and her daughter, Teresa, rush to grab clean clothes on May 17, 2000. Residents were only allowed forty-five minutes to gather belongings. Although many homes burned to the ground, the Sandoval's home remained unaffected.

Traffic leaves Los Alamos on New Mexico Highway 502.
The NPS recommended an evacuation for residents of the west side of town.

government officials could set such a huge fire so near their homes? What was being done to stop the fire? Who was going to pay for the resulting damages?

Bandelier Manager Roy Weaver stepped forward to take the blame. He said that he felt conditions were safe enough for the controlled burn. Far from calming the residents of Los Alamos, Weaver's comments served as a lighting rod for even more rage and criticism.

Fire crews continued to fight the flames, focusing on the area west of Los Alamos. By Tuesday they had burned blacklines in attempts to contain about 20 percent of the fire. Helicopters dumped a constant stream of water, and air tankers released orange fire retardants. Firefighters worked nonstop in the scorching heat to control the blaze.

The Fire Explodes

On Wednesday, May 10, 2000, the Cerro Grande Fire exploded.

Residents hoping to return to their Los Alamos homes stop at a National Guard checkpoint. Guard members escorted residents to those areas most heavily damaged.

Houses burn as the sun sets over Los Alamos. The skeleton of a fire-gutted truck contains propane tanks that somehow did not explode in the fire.

Winds reaching speeds of 50 miles per hour (80 km/h) howled out of the west, blowing flaming cinders for more than a mile (1.6 km) downwind. The fire easily crossed the blacklines and kept going. In hours, the blaze grew from 3,700 acres (1,500 ha) to more than 18,000 acres (7,300 ha). Huge billows of smoke rose from spot fires deep in the heart of Los Alamos Canyon. With that last line of defense gone, officials ordered the evacuation of Los Alamos.

Most residents of the town expected the call. Police and fire officials went from house to house urging people to leave. Soon a column of cars, packed with people and their most precious possessions, was streaming down the highway, headed toward the bigger cities of Santa Fe and Albuquerque, both to the south.

Within four hours, the remaining residents left Los Alamos. Only

"Questionable Judgment"

"The National Park Service as an institution bears substantial responsibility for the Cerro Grande Fire. . . . While the Board found no violations of policy on the part of individuals, questionable judgment was exercised on several occasions. The prescribed fire program should not be judged by the events of the Cerro Grande Fire. The lessons learned and the subsequent changes in management of the program will clearly serve to make it more effective in future applications."

— Cerro Grande Prescribed Fire Board of Inquiry Final Report

An aerial view of Los Alamos shows the erratic pattern of fire destruction.

emergency crews and news media remained. National Guard troops patrolled the deserted streets to prevent looting. Early the next morning, officials evacuated thousands of inhabitants of nearby White Rock.

While NPS firefighters tried to control the wildfire, Los Alamos Fire Department crews battled to save their town. Even New Mexico Governor Gary Johnson helped fight the fire, donning Nomex® clothing to take action on a small blaze near a house in Los Alamos. A 100-foot (30 m) wall of flame swept up from the south, sweeping out of the mesas and canyons and into the city's outskirts.

Crews fought to save businesses, homes, and schools but strong winds drove the fire. Firefighters fell back again and again before the blaze. Soon fire engulfed the city's southwestern neighborhoods and spread throughout the town. By the end of the day, two hundred sixty homes lay in ashes, and

33,000 acres (13,000 ha) of Los Alamos were blackened.

At Los Alamos National Laboratories, a bigger threat emerged. Environmentalists worried that if the fire destroyed the facility, it could release radioactivity. Special crews at the lab fought to keep the fire from getting near nuclear storage facilities. Even so, the flames came within 300 yards (274 meters) of a plutonium storage area. U.S. Energy Secretary Bill Richardson assured the nation that the facility could withstand a blaze without leaking radioactivity into the environment. But his words did little to comfort Americans.

The day after the fire exploded, President Bill Clinton declared Los Alamos and the areas surrounding the Cerro Grande Fire a national disaster area. That meant residents could apply for federal money to help rebuild their homes and businesses.

Clinton's ruling also meant that the Federal Emergency Management Agency (FEMA) could step in and begin to provide food and housing assistance to victims of the fire.

Not much is left to salvage as a fire victim surveys the devastated ruins of his home on May 14, 2000.

Uncle Sam the Arsonist?
"People do not pay their taxes for Uncle Sam to burn down neighborhoods."

— U.S. House Representative Jay Inslee

Red Cross volunteers Judy and Dick Opsahl view the remains of their home.

A National Uproar

The devastation at Los Alamos turned the Cerro Grande Fire from a regional problem to a national controversy. Television stations in New Mexico provided nonstop coverage of the blaze. Government officials — including Secretary Richardson, New Mexico's senators and the chief of the National Forest Service — flocked to the area to view the destruction.

Congressmen called for an official investigation into how the fire got so out of hand. Republican lawmakers bitterly criticized the Democratic Clinton administration for its controlled-burn policy. The U.S. House of Representatives unanimously passed a resolution that the federal government should take complete responsibility for the Cerro Grande Fire.

The Department of Interior and the NPS moved quickly to quiet the uproar. Roy Weaver, the Bandelier National Monument manager, was placed on leave during the investigation. Interior Secretary Bruce Babbitt announced that his department would look into the cause of the wildfire. Babbitt also declared a thirty-day suspension of prescribed burns for the entire West.

By Sunday, May 14, the Los Alamos fires had been put out and most of the town's residents were allowed to return home — except that many people no longer had a home. The flames burned a random path through the community. In one area, a single house was left intact while the surrounding ones were destroyed. Little pockets of destruction marked the town in odd places. Gas and electricity was still out in many parts of town, but people went back to work.

Even though the disaster was over for Los Alamos, the Cerro Grande Fire continued to burn for three more weeks. On June 6, 2000, the NPS officially declared the fire contained —

which meant that while it still burned in places, it was no longer spreading.

In the end, the fire destroyed almost 48,000 acres (19,000 ha) of forest land and destroyed or damaged two hundred eighty homes. The blaze caused $1 billion in damage. About six hundred families had no place to live; many had lost everything they owned. Overall, more than two thousand firefighters and support crews had battled the blaze.

The fire burned nearly 8,000 acres (3,200 ha) at Los Alamos National Laboratory alone, but air monitoring equipment recorded no release of radioactivity. The nearby Santa Clara Pueblo Reservation was hard hit — flames consumed more than 10 percent of the Reservation's land. Fire burned the banks and ash contaminated the water of a creek the residents depended on for fresh water.

Cerro Grande was only the beginning of a long nightmarish fire season. With widespread drought and record high temperatures, thousands of fires broke out in ten western states — sometimes as many as three hundred new fires a day. More than 4 million acres (1.6 million ha) of land were destroyed. At the height of the fire season, twenty-five thousand firefighters from the United States, Canada, and Mexico helped fight the blazes. More than two thousand members of the military also aided the fire crews. The cost of fighting all these fires came to almost $15 million per day.

By the time all the fires were out, much of the American West was a smoking wasteland. As area residents tried to clean up the mess, the rest of the nation tried to figure out how things had gone so terribly wrong.

Chapter 4

Learning to
Live With Fire

For the wilderness around Los Alamos, it was the beginning of a long struggle back to health. In the weeks after the fire, federal and state agencies created a Burned Area Emergency Rehabilitation (BAER) team. The team included biologists, archeologists, ecologists, and geologists. The BAER team organized thousands of volunteers who helped clean up after the fire.

The biggest task faced by the BAER team was protecting the devastated area from water runoff. With so many trees and undergrowth burned away, little remained to stop the heavy seasonal rains expected in July. Officials feared that flash floods might destroy much of the land and property that had

Fire silhouettes a swing set on property near Trinity and 48th Street in Los Alamos on May 11, 2000.

"Hotshot" team members from Zuni, New Mexico, continue their fight with smoldering areas of the fire.

survived the fire. Volunteers spread straw and seeded burned areas with fast-growing grass to act as a brake on floodwaters. They also built terraces and improved drainage areas to head off flooding. They raked up scorched soils that could no longer absorb water. They even filled twenty thousand sandbags to build temporary walls to hold back floodwaters.

At Los Alamos National Lab, workers shipped truckloads of radioactive dirt to an area that was protected from erosion. The soil they dug up was not newly radioactive — this was soil that had been contaminated by liquid radioactive

"We Must Use the Lessons Learned"

"The Cerro Grande Prescribed Fire had tragic results. Employees at all levels of the NPS, including the management and staff at Bandelier National Monument, have expressed deep regret for the impact it had on the lives of those people in Los Alamos who experienced property loss. We can and must gain from this experience. We must use the lessons learned as a basis to improve and enhance the prescribed fire program throughout the country and all agencies, for indeed we will need to continue to employ these methods to protect life and property in the future."

— Cerro Grande Prescribed Fire Board of Inquiry Final Report

Smoke from the Los Alamos fire was so dense it blocked the Sun.

waste since the 1940s. With so many of the surrounding trees and ground cover burned away, experts feared that floodwaters would wear away soil that had laid still for decades. Officials at the lab insisted there was no danger, but residents downstream continued to worry about radiation that might be getting into their drinking water.

After trucking away the toxic soil, Lab crews brought clean dirt to replace it. They lined nearby streams with rocks to minimize erosion.

While volunteers in New Mexico tried to deal with the fire's aftermath, legislators in Washington, D.C., struggled with the political fallout. The Department of Interior released the results of its investigation of the fire. The report concluded that fire planners had underestimated how complex the situation was in the proposed burn zone. Their report was particularly critical of Mike Powell for not getting backup fire crews to the scene fast enough. Had more firefighters been on the scene earlier, the report said, the fire might not have raged out of control.

A second report, by the Government Accounting Office (GAO), criticized the decision to burn at all. The GAO report pointed out that the area had been in the middle of a three-year drought at the time of the fire and that other prescribed fires in the region had also gotten out of control. With Los Alamos so close, the Cerro Grande Fire should never have been set in the first place, the report concluded.

In Congress, lawmakers continued to debate the wisdom of controlled burns. The Department of Interior responded by prolonging the ban on controlled burns. The Clinton Administration also adopted a national fire plan requiring counties in high-risk fire areas to develop formal fire plans, and to widen roads in forest areas so fire equipment could get through.

When George W. Bush began his presidency in 2001, the debate over

Missing Hard Drives

As workers at the Los Alamos National Laboratory returned to clean up after the fire, a startling discovery blew up into another national controversy. Two computer hard drives that held top-secret nuclear weapons information were missing. For two weeks, fifty-eight FBI agents investigated the loss while some members of Congress proclaimed that the nuclear secrets had been sold to the Chinese.

In the end, the drives turned up behind a copy machine, in an area that had already been searched. Investigators thought that someone who had taken the drives had tried to replace them without getting caught. The FBI found no evidence that the disappearance had anything to do with spying.

wildfires quieted down. But in 2002, the issue roared back to life. A small campfire in Colorado's Pike National Forest turned into a major disaster thanks to high winds and dry conditions. More than 100,000 acres (40,000 ha) went up in smoke. The fire crept to within 30 miles (48 km) of the city of Denver. The fire was the start of another major fire season with hundreds of firefighters battling blazes across the West.

Once again, people wanted someone to blame for the disaster. Experts pointed to the fact that decades of fire prevention left much of the West vulnerable to major fires. Now, people began to criticize the government for letting all this dry fuel build up. Congressmen and media analysts said it was time for the National Forest Service and other federal agencies to get more aggressive with controlled burns.

The debate about what to do about forest fires burns on. Every year, the

Greg Wilson photographs spoiled food in his refrigerator for insurance purposes on May 16, 2000.

issue becomes more critical. There are ten times as many homes in areas at risk of wildfire than there were just twenty-five years ago. In Colorado alone, nearly a million people live in areas that are vulnerable to fire.

In addition to controlled burns, some experts are proposing other solutions to the fire problem. These experts say that people should not be able to get fire insurance if they refuse to keep trees and other flammable material far away from their homes.

Others are pushing communities to limit the number of housing permits they issue in fire-prone areas.

One of the most controversial proposals is to let logging companies cut more trees in national forests in exchange for clearing out dead, dry trees and brush. Proponents say this would be an inexpensive way to reduce fire risk. But some environmental groups say that logging companies would damage the very habitats the policy is trying to save. They claim that

"Can We Learn to Live in the Woods?"

"These catastrophic fire seasons are going to become the norm. The question is, what are we going to do about it? Can we learn to live in the woods, when in most of these areas there aren't even building codes?"

— Bruce Babbitt, former Secretary of the Interior, talking about the 2002 fire season

Smoke hangs in the air as a firefighter trudges through the forest.
Many homeowners expect state and federal governments to protect them from fire.

"Remember Los Alamos!"

"Los Alamos and the surrounding communities suffered appalling losses in a disaster of the first order. But I am confident that they will rebuild stronger and better than before. The fire department, law enforcement, and emergency personnel who experienced this incident firsthand are all heroes. As for me and my team, we have shared in a piece of history that we will pass on to our grandchildren. We will certainly 'remember Los Alamos!'"

— Jim Paxon,
fire information officer
for the Cerro Grande Fire

Renea Anderson consoles her daughter, Nicole, at a Mother's Day church service for the victims of the Cerro Grande Fire.

firestorms have raced through areas that have already been logged.

While the debate goes on, more and more people move into what was once wilderness. These new homeowners expect their state and federal government to protect them from fire. The question of whether or not forest officials should set fires to prevent bigger fires remains.

As the fire at Los Alamos wildfires proved, the question about what to do with fire grows more urgent every day.

Time Line

1905	National Forest Service is formed to protect U.S. forest reserves.
1910	The Big Blowup destroys more than 3 million acres (1.2 million ha) of land and causes the Forest Service to adopt a policy of putting out all fires.
1995	U.S. government adopts a new fire policy calling for the use of prescribed burns.
2000	May 4: National Park Service crews start a controlled burn at Cerro Grande Peak in Bandelier National Monument, New Mexico.

May 5: Prescribed fire gets out of control; blaze is officially declared a wildland fire.

May 10: High winds cause the fire to quadruple in size in just a few hours; Los Alamos is evacuated.

May 11: President Bill Clinton declares Los Alamos a federal disaster area.

June 6: Cerro Grande Fire is declared contained. |

Glossary

adobe a sun-dried type of clay-and-straw building material used for homes in the American Southwest.

air tanker an airplane that carries water or fire retardants in large tanks.

archeologists scientists who study the remains of past life and cultures.

Bambi the classic animated Disney movie first released in 1942 featuring the life of a male fawn; includes a forest fire and the untimely death of Bambi's mother to a party of deer hunters.

blacklining containing a fire by burning anything around it that could serve as fuel for the blaze.

contaminate to make unfit for use.

controlled burn a fire — often with controlled boundaries — sometimes set as part of a wildlife management plan.

ecology the study of the interaction of living organisms and their environment.

environment the physical surroundings of a living organism; also refers to the natural world itself.

fire boss the head of a firefighting team.

fire retardant a chemical that stops a fire from spreading by robbing it of oxygen.

firestorm a fiery "weather" pattern created when hot air rising from a large fire causes surrounding air to rush in near the ground, feeding the flames with oxygen and making the fire burn even hotter and more furiously.

habitat the area where a plant or animal normally lives.

Manhattan Project the top-secret U.S. government project to develop an atomic bomb before the Germans and end WWII.

mesa a mountain or large hill with a broad, flat top.

napalm jellied gasoline.

Nomex® a special brand of fabric used for making fire-retardant clothing.

plutonium a highly radioactive by-product of nuclear power reactors that can be used to make nuclear weapons.

prescribed burn a fire planned by forestry management, often set to clear out dried timber and undergrowth.

propaganda ideas or information meant to change or influence opinion.

Pueblo/pueblo the name for a community of Southwestern Native Americans; also a and style of house commonly used in the Southwest.

radiation ionizing (harmful) energy or particles given off by unstable atoms as they break down.

radioactive a substance or object that gives off radiation.

ravine a narrow valley with steep sides, usually formed by water runoff.

suppressant an agent that stops or at least lessens the effects of something else.

timber a name for trees, particularly those grown for lumber or pulpwood.

wildland fire the official name for a fire in a forest or grassland that has gotten out of control.

For More Information

Books

The Big Burn. Jeanette Ingold (Harcourt)

Fire on the Mountain: The True Story of the South Canyon Fire. John N. Maclean (Washington Square Press)

Jumping Fire: A Smokejumper's Memoir of Fighting Wildfire. Murry A. Taylor (Harvest)

Secrets of a Los Alamos Kid 1946–1953. Kristin Embry Litchman (Los Alamos Historical Society)

Year of the Fires: The Story of the Great Fires of 1910. Stephen J. Pyne (Viking Penguin)

Videos

Fire: In the Heat of the Blaze. (A&E Entertainment)

Nova: Fire Wars. (WGBH Boston)

Raging Planet: Fire. (Discovery)

Take a Closer Look: Fire and the Longleaf. (Laurel Hill Press/Natural History Video Story)

Wildfires: Fighting Fire with Fire. Investigative Reports. (series) (A&E Entertainment)

Web Sites

Albuquerque Tribune – Cerro Grande Fire Area
www.abqtrib.com/archives/fire/051100_firemap.shtml

Federal Emergency Management Agency — Cerro Grande Fire Assistance Program
www.app1.fema.gov/cerrogrande/cg_00r46.htm

Los Alamos National Laboratory — Cerro Grande Fire Information
www.lanl.gov/worldview/news/fire/fire.shtml

National Park Service — Cerro Grande Fire
www.nps.gov/band/fire.htm

The Smokey Bear Web Site
www.smokeybear.com

USDA Forest Service Fire and Aviation Management Web Site
www.fs.fed.us/fire

Index